POSTMOD

Lacan and Postfeminism

Elizabeth Wright

Series editor: Richard Appignanesi

Published in the UK in 2000
by Icon Books Ltd., Grange Road,
Duxford, Cambridge CB2 4QF
email: info@iconbooks.co.uk
www.iconbooks.co.uk

Published in the USA in 2001
by Totem Books
Inquiries to: Icon Books Ltd.,
Grange Road, Duxford,
Cambridge CB2 4QF, UK

Distributed in the UK, Europe,
Canada, South Africa and Asia
by the Penguin Group:
Penguin Books Ltd.,
27 Wrights Lane,
London W8 5TZ

In the United States,
distributed to the trade by
National Book Network Inc.,
4720 Boston Way, Lanham,
Maryland 20706

Published in Australia in 2001
by Allen & Unwin Pty. Ltd.,
PO Box 8500, 9 Atchison Street,
St. Leonards, NSW 2065

Library of Congress catalog
card number applied for

Series editor: Richard Appignanesi

ISBN 1 84046 182 9

Typesetting by Wayzgoose

Printed and bound in the UK by
Cox & Wyman Ltd., Reading

Introduction: Poststructuralism and Postfeminism

Most definitions of postfeminism begin by piously asserting what it does not mean – that feminism is 'post' in the sense of past. Rather, the issue is one of a strategic move made by feminism: as a consequence of wanting women to band together collectively, feminists neglected the critique of a positive and stable identity. They relied on a stable concept of what a woman was, which led to 'essentialist' dilemmas, instead of subjecting 'woman' to critical analysis. Here they ignored that element in poststructuralism which focused on the ideological constructions of discourse.

Poststructuralism reacted against the binary oppositions of linguist Ferdinand de Saussure's theory,[1] in that it concentrated on discourse, in what happens in dialogue, rather than on language, what is in the dictionary. Saussure introduced the terms 'signifier' and 'signified' as two elements of the sign: the signifier is the sound image of a word, and the signified the concept corresponding to it. In itself this suggests a somewhat rigid conception of language, particularly since Saussure saw

The Political Minefield
1. The positive reading of postfeminism

Postfeminism has begun to consider the question of what the postmodern notion of the dispersed unstable subject might bring it. The term 'post-feminism' itself drags along its own problems of definition, both positive and negative.

The positive runs as follows. Postfeminism is continuously in process, transforming and changing itself. It does not carry with it the assumption that previous feminist and colonialist discourses, whether modernist or patriarchal, have been over-taken, but that postfeminism takes a critical position in relation to them.[3] This includes a challenge to 'second wave' feminism, that splendid, multiple and contradictory movement that surged across America, Britain and Europe, which eventually threatened to congeal through its assumptions that patriarchy and imperialism were at the root of all evil. This second wave in America and Britain took off with the student movements of the 1960s and thus preserved a dominantly polit-ical cast. Just as the first wave in the early decades of the 20th century strove towards the vote, the second focused on issues of equal rights at work, release from sexual and domestic control, and the critique of patriarchal ideology. In America, the leading lights were Betty Friedan, Kate Millett and Shulamith Firestone; in Britain these were Juliet Mitchell, Germaine Greer and Eva Figes. In its train this movement brought theoretical analyses which questioned patriarchal assumptions in attitude and practice. The emphasis upon collective action soon revealed internal strains through its neglect of difference, first of class and colour, and ultimately of identity. In part as a consequence, postfeminism began to participate in the discourse of postmodernism since it destabilises any notion of a fixed and whole-some subject, but it does so in unexpected and contrary ways.

French feminisms – and already we are in the world of the plural – approached the feminist movement with a key critical concept, that of *écriture féminine*. Although *écriture* straightforwardly means 'writing', a problem of translation immediately arises because *'féminine'* may be translated as either 'female' (and suggest nature) or 'feminine' (and suggest culture), whereas in French this problematic distinction can be side-stepped. The impulse of a feminine form of writing is to inscribe what it is to be feminine. Its exponents, round about the mid-1970s, asserted that in the so-called 'phallocentric' order of language, dubbed 'the male symbolic', there is no place for a feminine practice of writing. Its most famous practitioner is Hélène Cixous, who eschews all theory as irreducibly phallocratic, and is therefore aligned with Derrida and mis-aligned with Lacan. Both she and Luce Irigaray place a problematic emphasis on the woman's body and the maternal body, a 'writing from the body' that restores to women the difference denied them in phallocentric discourse. Cixous, in stressing the subversiveness of writing the fem-inine, is more in line with another important post-structuralist, the semiotician and psychoanalyst Julia Kristeva. Kristeva conceptualises a pre-Oedipal space where bodily pulsations, not yet gathered into a system of drives, will intermittently disrupt symbolic discourse; these pulsations Kristeva calls the 'semiotic'. Kristeva, however, is quite clear that the 'semiotic' makes itself felt in flows in constant motion, irrespective of whether their site is a male or female body. In fact, feminists are uneasy that her investigations into literature and poetry centre mainly on male avant-garde artists. None of these French feminisms align themselves with the feminist movement as it appeared in the Anglophone world, although their aims have their own political force. Despite their own critique of psychoanalysis, they were far more in tune with the notion of an unconscious than the Anglophone feminist world at that time. Their investigation of the complexities of subjectivity has eased the feminist transition into postmodernism.

2. The negative reading

The negative reading would insert a hyphen between 'post' and 'feminism'. It assumes that feminism is being sabotaged by the 'post', which indicates that feminism can now be dispensed with, at least in the form of making a special plea for the subjectivity of the feminine subject.

Although these so-called 'postfeminists', which include Naomi Wolf, Katie Roiphe, Rene Denfeld and Natasha Walter, are often labelled 'anti-feminist', they characterise themselves as precursors of a shift in aims and objectives of feminism: what some term a 'third wave'. Generally, they support an individualistic liberal agenda rather than a collective and political one, on which grounds their detractors frequently attack them for being pawns of a conservative 'backlash' against feminism, which seeks to limit its effectiveness.[4]

Rene Denfeld launches an indictment against a more senior group of feminist theorists whom she dubs 'The New Victorians', the main title of her book, and with whom she takes powerful issue.[5] She identifies the aspects of the 'old feminist order' and calls it puritanical (Catherine MacKinnon for her attack on the very idea of 'consensual sex'), conservative (Andrea Dworkin for her campaign against pornography), and weirdly New Age (Mary Daly for her fervent call to 'goddess worship'). She expresses disquiet that these issues under these influential names are given so much prominence on women's studies courses. In her chapter entitled 'The Antiphallic Campaign', she distances herself from feminist theorists who claim that heterosexuality is oppressive, and from the position that to be a lesbian is the most radical form of being a feminist rather than a sexual orientation as plausible as any other. In particular, she opposes the feminist conception of male bias as rooted in one global institution, that of patriarchy:

Following the widely accepted characterisation of society as 'patriarchy', today's feminists have created sweeping theories that effectively lump men together in one undifferentiated class. Patriarchy means 'the rule of fathers' but in today's movement the term is used with reckless abandon and applied to every aspect of society that current feminists dislike.[6]

Since, as we shall see, these very presuppositions are taken right into the core of Lacan's theory, it is important to pick them up in another context.

Why Psychoanalysis?

It was in Britain that Freudian and Lacanian psychoanalysis was taken up as a powerful aid in the discourse of women's liberation and rescued from the negative responses of leading feminists such as Betty Friedan, Kate Millett, Germaine Greer and others, who read Freud reductively, as a biological essentialist. Feminist writer and activist Juliet Mitchell, later also a psychoanalyst, argued that Freud's and Lacan's position on sexual difference was descriptive rather than prescriptive, that they showed up the conditions of patriarchy rather than promoted them. For Mitchell, Freud's theories of the unconscious and sexual difference show how desire is channelled to reproduce patriarchal power relations, how women are subjected to patriarchy. Psychoanalysis thus becomes a useful tool for an ideological analysis which can provide a basis for collective political action against women's oppression. In her introduction to *Feminine Sexuality*,[7] Mitchell first restates her former position:

To Freud, if psychoanalysis is phallocentric, it is because the human social order that it perceives refracted through the individual human subject is patrocentric. To date, the father stands in the position of the third term that must break the asocial dyadic unit of mother and child. We can see that this third term will always need to be represented by someone or something.

In the second introduction to this book, Jacqueline Rose takes the case for Lacan onwards by giving a detailed and lucid account of his theory of the subject divided in language. It becomes clear, then, that the 'third term' referred to above is represented by a particular symbolic position rather than a particular sexed person.

In my essay, Lacan's reading of Freud will be centred on his formulaic exposition of how the human subject comes to be either one sex or the other. Lacan deals with this problematic in his seminar, *On Feminine Sexuality, the Limits of Love and Knowledge: Encore*, in a section entitled 'A Love Letter'.[8] This section is included (in a different translation) in Mitchell and Rose's collection, but significantly this is the only chapter in the book which does not get a headword to help steer the reader through the difficulties of Lacan. It is to discuss a revolutionary interpretation of these formulae that this essay will be turning. Mitchell's account of Freud and Lacan was a brilliant intervention at its specific historical moment, but the widespread and continued allegiance to this view by feminists holds back what Lacan can bring to postfeminism.

The Post-Freud Wars

Both Freud and Lacan have been much misrepresented, not only in the psychoanalytic clinic and the academy, but also in the popular press. Clinically, both have been dismissed by many feminisms as damaging to the cause of woman for what are regarded as sexist and hetero-sexist theories of femininity. Even where they are given credit for a theory of the unconscious and of sexuality, it is of a grudging kind. Freud continues to be arraigned for his commitment to penis envy and to the Oedipus and castration complexes, Lacan for his rereading of Freud in terms of the centrality of the phallus and the symbolic function of paternity. Many feminists who otherwise do distinguished work will repeat the prime charges laid against both without troubling to struggle with Lacan's undoubtedly difficult texts, or if they do, they will still make their choice from the *Écrits* instead of looking at what else has been published by now.[9]

Many Freudian and Lacanian key concepts have been appropriated in the broad context of cultural studies, sometimes fruitfully, sometimes to their detriment. At the same time, feminist psychoanalytic criticism has become an ever-expanding field. Feminist interventions in the production and reception of the arts have made a distinct contribution towards revealing art to be a cultural practice that has historically excluded the subjectivities of women. Feminist literary and art criticism, and especially feminist film criticism, have a particular investment in exploring sign systems in order to find out how woman comes to be positioned in preordained social roles – daughter, wife, mother – within the restrictions of an inherited patriarchal circuit.

One of the currents of feminist psychoanalytic criticism that produced strong feelings in the 1980s took its impulse from object-relations theory, particularly with regard to relations between women, most notably those of mothers and daughters. Running counter to Freudo-Lacanian theory, object-relations (deriving from the psychoanalysts Melanie Klein and D.W. Winnicott) took as its themes plenitude rather than lack, connection rather than castration, celebrating what it saw as pre-Oedipal closeness between mother and infant rather than Oedipal loss. This had repercussions in the clinical world. In a recent collection called *Women Analyze Women*, female analysts have come to question the specificity of the female-to-female encounter, asking whether more primitive layers of experience could be uncovered in the situation of same-sex bodies than with a female/male couple.[10] Although nothing conclusive has emerged from this investigation, the topic has not been laid to rest.[11]

Psychoanalysis is currently the only discourse offering a theory of the unconscious. Hence it has been, and still is, of crucial interest for feminists and indeed all those who want to place themselves outside a rigid definition of sexual difference. The unconscious, however theorised, is the ground from which such rigid definitions can be challenged and transformed. Apart from those feminists who have merely passed on what they saw as bad news, there have also been women who have undertaken systematic critiques of Freud's repeated efforts to define femininity,[12] as well as analysts and feminists who have made distinguished contributions with their revisions of Freud in their clinical work or in their critique of the arts.[13]

Sexual Difference

For a considerable time, contemporary Western feminism remained confident regarding its sex/gender distinctions, its analysis of patriarchy, and its theory of the objectification of women under the 'male gaze'. These categories began to be undermined by the postmodern 'deconstructive' focus on the subject as unstable and dispersed. Lacan's reading of Freud has always moved in that direction, in a trajectory that travelled from structuralism with its emphasis on structure, to poststructuralism with its emphasis on textuality (the effects of one text upon another), to postmodernism with its emphasis on deconstruction.

Feminist reaction to psychoanalysis followed this route, always returning to the problem of femininity and feminine sexuality, moving uneasily between the poles of biology and culture. The problem is always that, in the Freudian universe of discourse, sexual difference can neither be reduced to a biological given nor be wholly constituted by social practices. A central part of the theoretical importance of psychoanalysis for feminism is its contention, now almost a cliché, that anatomy alone does not determine one's sexual identity, any more than sexual difference can be reduced to the cultural. So, if male/female sexualities are not essential categories and masculine/feminine not merely historical constructs, what produces sexual difference?

For Freud, what produces sexual difference is the meaning he assigned to anatomical differences of the male and female organs, when interpreted in terms of presence and absence. As a

17

castration /
lach

consequence, neither sex is complete: females suffer from 'penis envy', males suffer from 'castration anxiety'. What has to be remembered along with this bald statement is that, for Freud, human sexuality is always psychosexuality, the sexuality of the subject of the unconscious. It is also crucial that psychoanalysis defines sexuality in terms of 'libido' and 'drive', which were certainly picked up by Melanie Klein, but then got lost on the way until the appearance of Lacan. Similarly, Freud's question, 'what does a woman want?', was incorrectly translated into an articulation of 'female' rather than 'feminine' desire, which once more returned woman to biology. So what has Lacan contributed to the analysis of sexual difference?

Sexuation: Lacan's Contribution

What is sexuation? It is the process by which we unconsciously 'choose' our mode of being as either feminine or masculine. The term 'sexual difference' is not in the theoretical vocabulary of either Freud or Lacan. Where Freud defines anatomical differences in terms of their psychic consequences, Lacan defines sexual position in

terms of getting a place in the social as sexed subjects. Lacan stresses that we are all speaking beings:
we speak and we have being. Every human
'being' is submitted to castration by language and
speech. Entering into a system of rule demands a
sacrifice. For Lacan, what is primary is the limitation imposed by language upon all speaking
beings, in that the body's motivation (the
Freudian drive) is denied full satisfaction. This
creates a subject split between its symbolic identity
and the body that sustains it, hence Lacan's enigmatic 'barred' subject, $. This obtains in all soci-
eties, whether male- or female-dominated, even
though, at least in certain Western historical discourses, it is the phallus that has served to sym-
bolise this limitation. Lacan calls this limitation
the 'phallic function', that of castration, equally
operative for both sexes, in contrast to Freud, for
whom the penis was primary as regards the part
played in the child's sexual identification.

The crucial feature of the Lacanian subject is
that it is alienated by its very entrance into language, a system which both conjoins and divides.
As soon as the subject is caught in the defining

network of the signifier, it is divided between fixed identifications and actual being. Access into the symbolic inevitably produces a split in the subject between the *moi*, the misrecognising consciousness, and the *je*, which only appears in the gaps of consciousness, such as in symptoms and slips of the tongue. For Lacan, alienation is a structural condition of subjectivity *per se*. The splitting of subjectivity produces a sexual division and bestows symbolic gender.

This is already a different account from that given by feminism. Although Lacan's development of Freud was initially hailed precisely for its decisive turn from biology-as-destiny to the constitution of the subject-in-language, his theory was soon distorted out of all recognition by the accusation that he was phallocratic, assigning the phallus a position of power. His various, somewhat enigmatic statements on Woman, and the emphasis in his earlier work on the signifier of the phallus as the mark of difference, soon became as contentious as Freud's various attempts at theorising femininity and his pronouncements on penis envy. Feminists of every colour still declare war on the phallus as master-signifier, irrespective of what or how it signifies. Even though they may well be aware that 'phallus' cannot simply be equated with the penis, they still object to the use of an emblem derived from that bit of a man's body. *conclusion ?*

There are good historical reasons for the use of the term 'phallus', in so far as the phallus has played the role of penis in the cultural fantasies and imagination of the West, from, for example, the ancient Greek Dionysian mysteries to the fantasies revealed in early psychoanalytical case-histories. Lacan's formulaic account of sexuation, however, to which we will now turn, cannot be confined to a specific culture. In these formulae, it becomes evident that the phallic function, the function of castration – the sacrifice demanded by the symbolic – applies in different ways to both sexes, that it is not the case that the woman has lost something which the man does not have to lose, and that neither sex can have or be everything.

With the publication of a complete translation of Lacan's seminar *Encore*,[14] there is no longer any excuse for those wishing to grapple for themselves with his elaboration of the feminine and masculine position in the sexuation process. Although, in his first theory of sexuality in the 1950s, Lacan, looking to Freud, focused on the role of the phallus as a distinguishing mark between the sexes, seeing man as wanting to *have* it and woman wanting to *be* it, he now relied on a completely different dynamic. This dynamic does not imply in any way that the two sexes can be regarded as complementary, as one quality against another, as the bestseller *Men are from Mars, Women are from Venus* – he in his 'cave'/she in her 'well' – would have it.[15] The being/having divide may give two clear types of sexual position, but this indicates no more than two imaginary modes of identification by means of which each sex denies castration. 'Waiving the phallus, rather than waving it, is the fate of man and woman alike.'[16]

For Freud, as has been noted, what was critical was the meaning ascribed to anatomical differences of male and female sexual organs, when interpreted in terms of presence and absence. As a consequence, neither sex feels complete: males

conclusion ?

go on suffering from castration anxiety, females from penis envy. This part of the Freudian doctrine has produced much incredulity and offence because it invited, and still invites, so literal an interpretation.

Lacan, by considering psychoanalysis as a sexuation process, takes psychoanalysis a step further. Yet his theory of sexuation, the origin and development of sexual difference within the field of language, has really not fared much better. The feminist critique of the phallus is based on a misunderstanding of what the sexuation process implies. *Her opinion*

Lacan's Symbolic Logic of Sexuation

The elaboration that follows is based on Chapters VI and VII of Lacan's seminar XX.[17] My aim is to show to what extent the feminist critique of the phallus is based on a misunderstanding of what the sexuation process implies.

Lacan's diagram, shown on page 25, borrows symbols from a modified form of the predicate calculus, the symbolic logic that explores the relation of sets to each other. What he is dealing with in this 'symbolic logic' is the application of binary definitions to a hitherto disorganised part of existence, in that boundaries are laid down where no boundaries had been before. The distinguishing of entities (things and persons) in sets is common to logic, mathematics, language and sexual difference. For logical distinctness to emerge, every entity (x) must be defined against what it is not.

The formulae show each group as embodying an existential and a universal proposition which are in a contradictory relation to each other. An existential proposition tells us something about a single x which can either exist or not exist ('There is an x that is red'/'There is no x that is red'). A universal proposition tells us something about all such x's or none of them ('All x's are red'/'No x's are red').

In the formulae below, the logic of sexuation divides the field of speaking beings into two. The variable, x, on both sides stands indifferently for any speaking being. It does not represent a specifically sexed being, merely a being that speaks. On both sides there is a failure of the symbolic, in

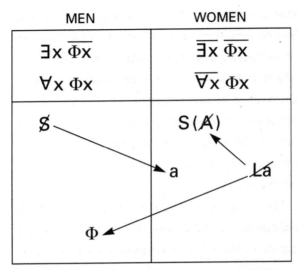

$\exists x$: 'There is at least one x.'

$\overline{\exists x}$: 'There is not a single x which . . .'

Φx: 'x is subject to the phallic function.'

$\overline{\Phi x}$: 'x is not subject to the phallic function.'

$\forall x$: 'All x's.'

$\overline{\forall x}$: 'Not all x's.'

a: The object a.

Φ: The phallic function.

$S(\cancel{A})$: The signifier of the barred Other.

$\cancel{La}$: indicates 'The Woman', who does not fall into a set, as she is not completely defined by the phallic function.

$\cancel{S}$: The barred Subject.

that the logic of language is inadequate for what it refers to, but it is a different failure for each side. The failure is about the degree to which *jouissance* (the Lacanian concept for the satisfaction of the drive*) is accommodated for each sex within any symbolic system.

In the top half of the graph there are four propositions, two existential ($\exists$) and two universal ($\forall$).

The male existential ($\exists x \overline{\Phi x}$) can be rendered as 'there is an entity x that says "no" to the phallic function'; the male universal ($\forall x \Phi x$) as 'all x's are subject to the phallic function'.

On the female side there are also two contrasting propositions: the female existential ($\overline{\exists x \overline{\Phi x}}$), 'there is no entity x that says "no" to the phallic function'; the female universal ($\overline{\forall x} \Phi x$), 'not all of x is subject to the phallic function'.

The phallic function (Φ) is the castration performed by the symbolic. As a product of this procedure, the phallus comes to signify the prohibited *jouissance* – the greater part of drive satisfaction that is forbidden to all subjects. This

*See a fuller definition in 'Key Terms' at the end.

sacrifice is demanded of men and women alike for entry into the symbolic, for subjecthood could not be achieved without setting limits to *jouissance*.

All speaking beings unconsciously insert themselves into this structure in whatever way they want, in line with their identifications, regardless of their biological sex. The variable, x, appears on both sides of the formula, which makes clear that there is only one category of speaking being, or that any speaking being can take up a position on one side or the other. Lacan makes this point explicit:

Any speaking being whatsoever, as is expressly formulated in Freudian theory, whether provided with the attributes of masculinity – attributes that remain to be determined – or not, is allowed to inscribe itself in this part [the female side].[18]

On the male side, there is an attempt to identify with the phallus, that is, to imagine oneself as the master who issues the prohibitions. But this is no more than a posture, even if it has real effects at any one historical time. The universal proposition states that all men fall under the phallic function, that is, must submit to symbolic castration.

This rule is guaranteed by virtue of an exception, namely the existential proposition, that there is one man who is exempt. The set of castrated beings can only be kept together if there is an exception. Lacan relates this exception to Russell's mathematical paradox, making the namer and gatherer of the set stand outside, not to be defined by what he is defining.[19] For Lacan, this exception to the rule is linked to the myth of the primal father in Freud's *Totem and Taboo*, who had made no sacrifice of his *jouissance*.[20] We can take this to represent the *illusion* upon which the symbolic works, that finally *jouissance* will be restored in full.

On the female side, woman is 'not-all' identified with the phallic function; she says yes *and* no, yes *or* no to it, the female formula demonstrating the undecidability and impossibility of totalising the woman. Femininity is not organised as a universal function, as is masculinity; hence 'not-all' the woman is subject to the phallic function. This does not mean that she is 'not at all' in the symbolic, but that there is no universal affirmation possible on the side of woman. The woman's side exists, but not as a defined set like that for man, and this is why Lacan uses the hyperbole 'The Woman does not exist'.

She has an additional possibility, as the lower diagram shows; she is bound to castration through being subject to the phallic function, but she is also related to the signifier of the barred Other, $S(\bar{A})$: 'A' stands for *Autre* (Other); the slash stands for a gap or lack in the Other – a recognition that the promised rewards of the symbolic are not guaranteed. Thus, as a consequence of not being entirely within the symbolic, she has a supplementary *jouissance*, one not related to the castration enjoined by the phallic function – a *jouissance* that castration forgets.

For the man, a surplus *jouissance* – what he is denied by castration – is trapped by what Lacan calls 'the object *a*'. This object is first felt as a lack in being by all subjects, an alienation consequent to entry into the symbolic, which the man deals with by seeking a fantasy in the woman. This search for a fantasy in the woman can take place equally between a biological man and a biological woman, between two biological men or between two biological women, as the above quotation from Lacan illustrates.

The phallic function applies to all, guaranteed by the one exception who appears as exempt from castration, the primal Father, and hence is the source of the law of castration that bears on the desires of all others. Since Woman, however, is not completely defined by the phallic function, 'The' is crossed out, indicating that she does not fall into a set. Hence, 'The Woman does not exist'.

This elaboration of Lacan's formulaic treatment of sexual difference is the only way to argue his case against the widespread accusation of being phallocentric, with the phallus always seen as a signifier of male power. Far from this being the case, each sex is lacking as a result of being in the symbolic, but it is not a penis they lack, even though the phallus is used as a metaphor and stands for the phallic function, that which divides the subject and thus creates the speaking being. The phallic function appears on both sides.

The logic of the sexuation formulae produces two sets of speaking beings not in a complementary relation to each other. Crucially, the formulae do not plot which sexual position a subject may take up – they are not *hetero*-sexuation formulae. What they reveal are the historical limits of the possibility of change. They are nothing to do with a particular subject's object-choice, which can go across biology. But however variable object-choice may be, society will still demand a binary of some kind, whatever the biology of human beings might become in the far-flung future. There will still have to be the equivalent of a 'castration', without which the entry into language would be foreclosed.

For Lacan, these formulae are concerned with how a speaking being experiences sexuality on the level of the psyche. They have nothing to do with biological sex, neither with the love of a man for a woman, nor that of a man for a man, nor that of a woman for a woman. This implies that a biological male can inscribe himself on the female side and a biological female on the male side. Each speaking being can choose to inscribe itself on either side, although this will be a 'forced' choice, imposed by the parameters of the history of the subject's unconscious.

Gender Arguments: Masquerade, Performance and Citation

What Lacan emphasises is the division between the organism and the subject, while at the same time recognising the continuity between the bodily and the psychic. A division between organism and subject removes the need to depend on a biological determination of gender, which always assumes a masculinity and femininity derived from the real body. To make this assumption is to give a position to those subjects who believe their body does not match the sexed identity of their choice, who ask for their bodies to be surgically changed.

In another key, the discordance of the subject 'normally' plays itself out in pretence and masquerade. In a celebrated paper, Joan Riviere, a distinguished analyst of the 1920s and 30s and a translator of Freud's work, maintains that womanliness is a cover-up to conform with social constructions of femininity, a masquerade whereby the woman as a category does not exist.[21] Riviere's patient used womanliness as a 'feint' or 'cover-up', for 'there is no absolute femininity beneath the veil, only a set of ontologically tenuous codes that normatively induct the female subject into the social practice of "being" woman through mimesis and parroting'.[22] The clinical example in Riviere's essay represents the female intellectual who excels at playing both a male and female role in her life. She followed a day spent after a successful public performance by a night seeking reassurance for what she felt to be inappropriate behaviour. She obtains this reassurance by being flirtatious and seductive. Thus, argues Riviere, womanliness could be put on both to hide the phallic position and to forestall reprisal for taking it up. But is there any distinction between womanliness and pretence? No, Riviere says, they are the same. There is a capacity for womanliness, but it can only manifest itself in this defensive way. Hence there is no essence of femininity, no 'eternal feminine' as immortalised in Goethe's *Faust*.

Riviere's paper has been taken up in various ways. The masquerade as Riviere defines it has been seen as a forerunner of Lacan's dictum 'The Woman does not exist', that is, in the unconscious there is no signifier for 'The Woman'.[23] The masquerade is not in the imaginary register (it is unlike display in animals), but in the symbolic one. As already noted, the sexes cannot be neatly divided into two complementaries, because the symbolic sexual distinction takes no account of the lack in the Other, that which invades the boundaries of language and speech, the real within and without mundane reality.[24] No division is ever going to fall neatly between masculine and feminine: each subject's desire will do it differently. Sexual difference always exceeds, is more than, gender difference. For example, let us consider Othello's comment on Desdemona: 'She loved me for the dangers I had passed;/And I loved her, that she did pity them.' She loves him *quoad castrationem* – in the form of a castrated being, because the history of his suffering makes manifest the inescapability of castration; he loves her *quoad matrem* – seen in

34

that works through a constitutive lack via
promise it cannot fulfil. Hence the Other wo
through a kind of deceit which, if not recogni
and capitalised upon, has catastrophic results
self and society.[30] The trap for feminism is
interpret this deceit as merely patriarchal dor
nation, when the challenge is to enter and enga
in the performance.

Judith Butler considers the position of t
wearer of drag. She argues that drag is not nec
arily subversive, since it is a parody which par
oxically can confirm heterosexual norms.
rag, there is an exaggerated miming of t
pposite sex, which Butler regards as a form
nder melancholia, an unconscious grief for t
ss of the same-sex person, a 'renunciation
possibility of homosexuality'.[31] In her view,
ows that drag enacts a heterosexual mela
ly, since the drag-artist is unable to grieve.
itler has no explanation of how such 'gend
ormativity' works. She uses the metaph
itation' (borrowed from Derrida[32]) in ord
xplain performativity. What is 'citation
ion is a quotation from another's words in

the form of a mother, offering consolation.[25] That
is why for Lacan, there is no such thing as a sexual
relationship.[26] The masquerade reveals a structure: it is a response, not to the man's desire, but
to a male fantasy, an identification with the
desire of the man in his fantasy.

Feminists have considered Riviere's term as a
kind of fetish of feminist discourse (taken up by
Irigaray, Montrelay, and feminist film critics) and
an obstacle in political critiques of femininity
seeking to abolish stereotypes of the feminine. At
the same time, in its emphasis on gender as performance, the concept of masquerade offers a way
out of biological essentialism, since anyone who
pleases can play the woman. As well as being
appropriated for theories of anti-essentialism, it
has also been influential in gender studies by theorists such as Judith Butler, discussed below, who
sees masquerade as a refusal of female homosexuality even while the masquerading subject is
incorporating the rejected female Other (initially
the mother).[27]

Riviere's original question has been reposed by
Slavoj Žižek, who asks whether, if a certain femi-

nist critique denounces every description of the feminine as a male cliché, what, then, is the feminine 'in itself'? The problem is that all of the answers from Kristeva to Irigaray can be discredited as male clichés. Feminist values of intimacy and attachment have been opposed to male ones of autonomy and competitiveness. The question is, are these feminine virtues authentic features or are they imposed by patriarchy? Žižek's answer is 'both at once'. Every positive determination, any attempt to define woman as an essence, as she is 'in herself', can only bring us back to what she is performing, what she is 'for the other': for 'it is precisely in so far as woman is characterised by an original masquerade, in so far as all her features are artificially "put on", that she is more subject than man'.[28]

The masquerade can be seen as a veiling of the lack, a hiding of its nothingness. Jacques-Alain Miller, the literary and intellectual inheritor of Lacan's work, cites the fact that men have always been fascinated by the covering-up of women, the imaginary 'semblance' that is preferred to the threat of the real lack that the removal of the veil

would reveal. 'We no doubt cover wome because we cannot discover Woman. We ca invent her.' He points to the women who possessions, presenting themselves as 'the who has' – the lost mother who possesse thing – and the men who collude wi enticed into the imaginary possession o possesses: 'Lacan loved to point out th tion *bourgeoise* given to the wife in p lance, as in *ma bourgeoise* ['my indicates that she is the one in charge finances.'[29]

In order to grasp the notion of m pertains to the specific predicame we have to move to the structure of the subject to the Other. Wh The Other in Lacanian thought of discourses such as social a cultural studies; it is not anothe In psychoanalysis, the Other i ally as the symbolic system i ual self in its autonomy is t The Other is not so much t reality and directs our ch

new context, and this inevitably produces a new meaning. What the notion of citation leaves out, however, is the explanation of this very process. It could be said that all utterance is a form of citation, since with every word we are quoting the language itself. The symbolic is only a ruse by which we refer to the being we have and that we experience.

It is Lacan's concept of the 'real' that provides the explanation, a key concept usually left out of dictionaries and glossaries to avoid the difficulty it poses. Any performance at all, be it art or life, has to partake of the real. What, then, is this 'real'?

The Real

The real is at once the curse and glory of any system, since it is both the possibility of holding such systems in place and of changing them. So much, both philosophy and psychoanalysis would agree on. In the academic discourse, the real often emerges as confused with 'reality' – the mundane world – whereas the 'real' is the ground from which 'reality' and its objects are selected by human trial and error. Lacan thus distinguishes what *exists* (the everyday reality of familiar objects) from what *ex-sists*, 'stands outside' (the real, the ground from which these things are chosen).

For the philosopher, in the wake of the pre-Socratic Heraclitus, the real is the continuum, the river which is not identical with itself and hence in which you never step twice. For the psycho-analyst, the relation of repetition to the real involves the invasion of consciousness by the unconscious. The relation of repetition to the real can be seen in the psychoanalytical transference, that emergence of unconscious wishes that takes place in the analytic encounter when the patient projects his past relations with significant others onto the analyst: 'what is repeated, in fact, is always something that occurs . . . *as if by chance*'.[33] Lacan here speaks of a 'missed encounter', a term which brings together, on one side, the under-lying being of experience (the 'encounter') and, on the other, the fact that it is not understood. It is not recognised because it is unrepresentable, unassimilable, and yet it is precisely this which triggers the repetitions. It is the task of analysis to discover how the real gets caught up in the machinic repetitions, geared as they are to the Other's expectations.

The real is only ever experienced, never wholly conceptualised; it is what words, concepts, percepts, apply to. Therefore, any separation produced by the symbolic, particularly in the earliest moments, will break into the chaotic experience of the infant and produce shock. To 'miss' the encounter is to fail to grasp the brute experience. The symbolic works upon the real by means of repetition, but never turns into it. Mundane reality awaits construction out of the real; however, the construction is not something that can be wholly altered at the whim of a subject, but it is still open to serious intervention.

Each use of a word in language is a repetition which hopes to capture a part of the real in the effort to establish an identity, this being a working principle of the symbolic, how it is to be performed. But since the real remorselessly invades these repetitions, performance takes on a particular character. Now we can see what Butler's 'citation' actually is. 'Citation' involves an incalculable private element and it is this which can make visible the 'deceit' of the symbolic. If the real is indeed that within which subjects carry out the performances that the symbolic has provided, then, as Lacan's formulae illustrate, the real will cross the binary of feminine and masculine unexpectedly within these constitutive repetitions.

Lacan and the Postfeminist Critique of the Cinema

Masquerade exemplifies the failure of the real to match the symbolic. It is an attempt by woman to negotiate her subjectivity within the constraints of the symbolic system in which she is included. Some feminist film theorists have seen it as a benign form of play; others see it as a pathological reaction to male dominance. In film theory, feminist thought and Lacanian theory come together. In their use of psychoanalytic theory, feminists have paid particular attention to the function of the image, the gaze, the producer and the spectator, for all of which the locus of the cinema may be regarded as paradigmatic. The conjunction of psychoanalysis and the cinema first emerged as a powerful form of ideological criticism in the mid-1970s and 80s.[34] This criticism announced itself in an early use of Lacan's concepts of the mirror phase and the imaginary, and his development of the Freudian drive and the split subject.

Much of 1970s' criticism took off from the work of Christian Metz, who theorised the contribution made by psychoanalysis to an understanding of how film and cinema worked at an unconscious level.[35] In particular, he discussed the way the 'scopic regime' of the cinema leads to mechanisms of voyeurism and fetishism: cinema becomes a desiring machine by bringing into play the 'scopic drive'. What is the scopic drive? In Lacan's rethinking of Freud, the gaze and voice are both first incorporated by the infant in concrete response to the mother's recognition of it; in Lacan's 'mirror phase', the mother is already implicated through being present in the infant's perception of itself, which includes being held. The result is a locating of the subject in the field of the Other, the social. From then on the scopic drive (associated with the eye) essentially involves the subject's constituting itself in relation to others: 'what is involved in the drive is making oneself seen (*se faire voir*). The activity of the drive is concentrated in this *making oneself (se faire)*'.[36] Thus, in the scopic fantasy the subject exists only in relation to an imaginary gaze, the (m)Other's.

With this notion of the gaze, feminist film criticism comes into force, but there is still a theoretical difficulty owing to the fact that feminist psychoanalytic film critics conflate a notion of the 'look' with that of the 'gaze'. The French term *'le regard'* serves for either, but the translators of Lacan use 'gaze', while those of Jean-Paul Sartre use 'look'. In Sartre's thinking, *le regard* (look) is on the side of the subject; while in Lacan's later thinking *le regard* (gaze) is on the side of the object, in the field of the Other.[37] Thus, it has to be made clear that in the discussion of what came to be known as the cinema's specular regime, the look is identified with the camera and the camera is on the side of the subject.

Psychoanalytic film criticism sees the cinema spectator as positioned by the cinematic apparatus, which includes a darkened room, larger-than-life figures overhead, and methods of classical editing which 'suture' the spectator into the filmic narrative in analogy with the Lacanian mirror phase. 'Suture' is a metaphor taken from surgery for the uniting of two body surfaces, especially the stitching together of the edges of a wound. According to Metz, the primary identification is with the spectator's own activity of looking, not with the persons on the screen. The cinematic signifier constructs a fetishistic relation for the spectator to the frame, the characters, the story, and even to the cinematic institution itself. Since in classical Hollywood cinema the camera is usually controlled by a male director, the spectator's perception is joined to the orchestration of the male look, which leads us to the point of feminist intervention.

Feminist film criticism came into its own with the appearance of a much-cited essay by Laura Mulvey[38] which inaugurated a strong feminist investment in questions of representation. She argued that the look is linked to the discovery of sexual difference, the woman's lack of a penis. In Hollywood cinema from the 1930s to the 50s, various glamorous images of women were destined to fill this lack, such that the woman becomes a substitute for the imaginary phallus, provoking and satisfying the male viewers' voyeuristic and fetishistic needs. As Mulvey formulated it, this makes the man the active bearer of the look and the woman its passive object.[39] In identifying with the camera held by a male director, the spectator identifies with the male look. The spectator is thereby sutured into the film from an unavoidably masculine voyeuristic position. An important corollary of this analysis was that she theorised pleasure as a negative term, a mark of the spectator's collusion with an oppressive sexual system. With the appearance of this article, the film became a feminist weapon *par excellence*, such that 'feminism and psychoanalysis became tools in an absorbing act of decipherment for Mulvey's film theory and for its discovery of "active spectatorship" which aimed to lay bare "the social unconscious under patriarchy"'.[40]

The late 1980s and early 90s, however, saw the launching of a late Lacanian critique of the use made of Lacan in Metz's and Mulvey's analyses, which now sees these analyses as grounded in a misconception of Lacan's notion of the gaze, as presenting the subject as too much determined by the image on the screen. A compelling case has been made that there is a problem concerning the screen conceived as a mirror (derived from the Lacanian mirror phase) and the mirror conceived as a screen (to be derived from a proper understanding of the Lacanian gaze).[41] This problem arises because the Lacanian gaze has been confused with the social historian Michel Foucault's 'panoptic gaze' which defines the perfect visibility of woman under patriarchy and 'of any subject at all'.[42] The panoptic apparatus of the 19th century denies the existence of what lies outside the visible and the known.[43] This is not to say that this apparatus ignores the fact that individual subjects are in conflict as to what constitutes knowledge, but rather that the apparatus assumes that a determinate knowledge, totally defined, can be arrived at as the outcome of such conflicts. The Lacanian system, to the contrary, shows that what is produced by a signifying system can *never* be determinate. Conflict here does not arise

47

from the conflict between two different positions, but from the fact that neither of them arises from a secure identity, that no definitive knowledge can be arrived at.

This new view of the cinema was radical to the extent that it rejected a theory of representation grounded in a reality presumed to be already there before the discourses which help to construct both it and the spectatorial subject. The concept of 'apparatus' came in the wake of Gaston Bachelard and Louis Althusser, who both traced discourses to their historical determinations. As a consequence, the imaginary dimension revealed in Lacan's mirror phase was taken as a necessary ideological founding of the subject, who was thereby seduced into an illusion of his/her own mastery of the image.

Postfeminist film theory has moved from Christian Metz's theorisation of the cinematic signifier as imaginary, to Lacan's theorisation of a dialectic between 'the eye' and 'the gaze'. In this theory, the eye is not merely an organ of perception but also an organ of pleasure. There is a 'dialectic of the eye and the gaze'[44] – 'the eye' as caught up in the symbolic order and 'the gaze' as pursuing a narcissistic fantasy – for every object, subjected as it is to the scopic drive, partakes of the conflict between imaginary fantasy and the demands of the symbolic, the desire of the Other. The speaking subject can never be wholly trapped in the imaginary, as earlier feminist film theory believed. The process that brings about the ideological operation of subject-construction cannot be assumed to work without any error.

For Lacan, misrecognition is inseparable from the very process of construction, for the subject can never locate itself at the point of the gaze. The visual field ceases to be a mirror and becomes a screen.[45] Hence, it is theoretically inadequate to concentrate on the spectator's imaginary identifications when the emergence of alterity disturbs the distinction between object and subject, 'between what "I" look at and what "I" am'.[46] The earlier film theory treated identification as recognition and thus missed the invasion of otherness. The cinematic illusion is no meaningless phantasmagoria, but is traversed by the signifiers that the ideology has released into the visual field. Yet these signifiers cannot be solely confined by that ideology. Where the Foucauldian view sees the signifiers as opaque to the subject, wholly monopolising its gaze, this very attention allows the subject to project beyond this opacity, to sense that which is missing in the mundane interpretations of the signifiers – the breakings-through of the ignored or 'impossible' real. The real is 'impossible' from the standpoint of the imaginary that the ideology has in its grip, but its existence makes itself felt all the more terrifyingly other, because of its absence from the spectator's illusory world. Therefore, the screen, instead of being merely a mirror for the narcissism of the subject, becomes a screen – an alien opaque element that meets and challenges the gaze of the subject.

The artist René Magritte's picture *Dangerous Relationships* can be used as a metaphor here. In the picture, a naked woman hides behind a mirror. But the mirror thus used as a screen betrays her desire to be seen, for in the mirror we see the back of the naked woman herself. She hides (masquerades) as feminine while wanting to be looked at as the phallus. She solicits the gaze by an affectation of modesty, but the screen/mirror not only does not conceal but reveals what it should not: that in her feminine masquerade she is phallic.

In line with these theoretical re-visions, feminist film criticism of the 90s has turned away from a central concern with the mechanisms of fetishism and voyeurism towards the constructions of fantasies and to what it takes to keep the dialectic of subject and Other constantly in view. One of the most recent and striking developments of feminist film criticism has been the attention paid to the *film noir*, a type of Hollywood film of the 40s and 50s, retrospectively made into a genre.[47] There are two aspects of this genre, which together make up its ideological appeal for feminists: one is its formal devices, the other its scenario. The formal devices articulate the enigmas proposed by the scenario. A *chiaroscuro* visual style of white light and black shade in an urban setting defines the mood for the duplicitous action whose motor is the *femme fatale*. How does the *film noir* position the spectator, and what fantasies does it have to offer through its devices, plot and characters? On the one hand, the film presents itself as a masculine genre. A male hero is struggling with other men trying to overcome alienation in a corrupt system, lured by a dangerously deceptive woman: 'the power accorded to the femme fatale is a function of fears linked to the notions of uncontrollable drives, the fading of subjectivity, and the loss of conscious agency – all emergent themes of psychoanalysis'.[48] So one way of looking at *film noir* is to see the woman's destruction by the plot or by the male hero as retribution for having aroused his passive desire, for having enthralled him with the promise of love, for entrapping him with her dangerous sexuality. On the other hand – and against seeing *film noir* as a specifically masculine genre – women take up active roles in these films, even and especially where their desire is sinister and they finally incur punishment. However, since the fantasy of the promiscuous woman is inscribed in the Oedipal scenario, the pleasures of the forbidden are shared by both feminine and masculine subjects.

This, then, runs counter to Mulvey's classic argument, that within patriarchy cinematic pleasure is invariably dominated by the male look; it is also governed by the woman's unconscious fantasy which partakes of the forbidden. For what becomes evident in *film noir* is that the *femme fatale*'s active desire manifests itself in her endeavour to draw the man into her circuit. The *film noir* epitomises the problem of masquerade, in that the woman as fantasy object is drawing on her phallic attributes to make herself desirable, but nevertheless this identification can also be an active place offered to the female spectator who can enjoy it deconstructively.

'The woman does not exist'

What, then, is a woman? A book entitled thus raises this very question.[49] It argues that the question of what a woman is can never have just one answer: woman is not a fixed reality, but her body is a place for her to pursue possibilities. This takes as a blueprint the Existentialist view of Simone de Beauvoir, who did not deny that biology is the fundamental ground of the human world. But for Beauvoir, 'the body is a situation',[50] part of the concatenation of historical circumstances out of which freedom has to be purchased. 'Becoming a woman' does not imply an opposition of sex and gender, but is the way a woman uses her freedom.

This does not mean that woman is not less complete than man, for man is whole only with respect to having wholly entered into phallic signification. Woman, on the other hand, lacks a signifier, and therefore has to use the subterfuge of masquerade. The importance of Riviere's essay lies in its questioning the distinction between genuine womanliness and pretence. Lacan's dictum, 'The woman does not exist', indicates that in the unconscious there is no signifier for 'the woman'. The masquerade reveals a psychical structure which is a response not to a man's desire but to a male fantasy. Moreover, biological differentiations are inadequate. Too many people seem to cross over: there are biological males with feminine structure and biological females with masculine structure. In Freud's ongoing questioning of what a woman wants, and Lacan's misunderstood sexuation theory, there is the insight that the feminine is not entirely determined by the phallic and that therefore woman is more a subject than man. What lived experience is about is the struggle to make something of 'the body as a situation'.

To develop this line of reasoning, a Lacanian feminism would imply a fundamental recognition of the singularity of the feminine element. In this sense, you could have a grouping across the categories of feminine/masculine/lesbian/gay/queer which might be politically active for whatever changes it wishes to promulgate. One of these might well be to allow for the emergence of a new 'master-signifier' to stand for the limitation of *jouissance*. It is well to remember, though, that any kind of categorisation is in danger of lending itself to a new form of hierarchical totalisation.

Postfeminism has begun to consider the question of what the postmodern notion of the dispersed unstable subject might bring it. As far as this brief study is concerned, the answer is Lacan, who has launched a powerful critique of stable identity without getting rid of it altogether. To get rid of it altogether would be to invite a psychotic exit from the symbolic, and Lacan always returns to the inescapable engagement with the symbolic, the subject's attempt to keep the real present within it. The split subject does not throw off its castration. Feminism can make use of this critique of positive identity, without deconstructing identity out of existence.

Notes

1. Ferdinand de Saussure, *Course in General Linguistics*, trans. Wade Baskin, eds. Charles Bally and Albert Sechehaye (London: Fontana/Collins, 1977), p. 113.

2. For a further explanation of the significance of Lacan's use of Saussure, see pp. 96–8 and pp. 184–8 in Dylan Evans, *An Introductory Dictionary of Lacanian Psychoanalysis* (London and New York: Routledge, 1996).

3. Ann Brooks, *Postfeminisms: Feminism, Cultural Theory and Cultural Forms* (London and New York: Routledge, 1997).

4. Sarah Gamble, ed., *The Icon Critical Dictionary of Feminism and Postfeminism* (Cambridge: Icon Books, 1999), pp. 298–9.

5. Rene Denfeld, *The New Victorians: A Young Woman's Challenge to the Old Feminist Order* (London and New York: Simon and Schuster, 1995).

6. Ibid., p. 30.

7. Juliet Mitchell and Jacqueline Rose, *Jacques Lacan and the École Freudienne: Feminine Sexuality*, trans. Jacqueline Rose (London and Basingstoke: Macmillan, 1982), p. 23.

8. Jacques Lacan, 'A Love Letter', in *The Seminar of Jacques Lacan: On Feminine Sexuality, the Limits of Love and Knowledge. Book XX. Encore: 1972–1973*, trans. Bruce Fink, ed. Jacques-Alain Miller (New York

and London: W. W. Norton & Co., 1998), pp. 78–89.

9. Jacques Lacan, *Écrits: A Selection*, trans. Alan Sheridan (London: Tavistock Publications, 1977a). See Kaja Silverman, 'The Lacanian Phallus', *Differences*, 4:1 (1992), pp. 84–115, as one who bases her view of Lacan mainly upon Lacan's 1958 essay 'The Signification of the Phallus', in *Écrits*, pp. 281–91. For a succinct and judicious reading of Lacan, see Darian Leader and Judy Groves, *Introducing Lacan* (Cambridge: Icon Books, 2000).

10. Elaine Hoffman Baruch and Lucienne J. Serrano, *Women Analyze Women: In France, England and the United States* (New York and London: Harvester-Wheatsheaf, 1988).

11. Joan Raphael-Leff and Rosine Jozef Perelberg, eds., *Female Experience: Three Generations of British Women Psychoanalysts on Work with Women* (London and New York: Routledge, 1997).

12. Sarah Kofman, *The Enigma of Woman: Women in Freud's Writings*, trans. Catherine Porter (Ithaca and London: Cornell University Press, 1980).

13. For Julia Kristeva, see particularly *Black Sun: Depression and Melancholia* (New York: Columbia University Press, 1989); for Hélène Cixous, see Hélène Cixous and Catherine Clément, *The Newly Born Woman*, trans. Betsy Wing (Manchester: Manchester University Press, 1986).

14. Lacan, 1998 (see footnote 8).

15. John Gray, *Men are from Mars, Women are from Venus: A Practical Guide for Improving Communication and Getting What You Want in your Relationships* (New York: HarperCollins, 1992).

16. Parveen Adams, 'Waiving the Phallus', *Differences*, 4:1 (1992), pp. 78–83.

17. Lacan, 1998, pp. 64–89; for the formula, see p. 73.

18. Ibid., p. 80.

19. Bertrand Russell, *The Principles of Mathematics* (London: Allen and Unwin, 1903), pp. 523–4.

20. Sigmund Freud, *Totem and Taboo, Standard Edition of the Complete Psychological Works, Vol. XIII*, ed. and trans. John Strachey (London: Hogarth Press and the Institute of Psycho-Analysis, 1940–68; *Totem and Taboo* originally published 1912), pp. 1–161.

21. Joan Riviere, 'Womanliness as a Masquerade', *International Journal of Psycho-Analysis*, 8 (1929), pp. 303–13.

22. Emily Apter, 'Masquerade' in *Feminism and Psychoanalysis: A Critical Dictionary*, ed. Elizabeth Wright (Oxford: Blackwell, 1999), pp. 242–4.

23. Jacques Lacan, *Television: A Challenge to the Psychoanalytic Establishment*, trans. Jeffrey Mehlman, ed. Joan Copjec (New York and London: W. W. Norton & Co., 1990), p. 38. See also Vincente Palomera, 'Womanliness as a Masquerade', *Lacanian Ink*, 5 (1992), pp. 43–51.

24. Jacques Lacan, '*Tuché* and *Automaton*' in *The Four Fundamental Concepts of Psycho-Analysis*, trans. Alan Sheridan, ed. Jacques-Alain Miller (London: Hogarth Press and the Institute of Psycho-Analysis, 1977b), pp. 53–64 (see pp. 53–6).

25. Lacan, 1998, p. 35.

26. Ibid., pp. 7 and 71.

27. Judith Butler, *The Psychic Life of Power: Theories in Subjection* (Stanford, California: Stanford University Press, 1997), pp. 132–50.

28. Slavoj Žižek, *The Indivisible Remainder: An Essay of Schelling and Related Matters* (London and New York: Verso, 1996), pp. 160–1.

29. Jacques-Alain Miller, 'On Semblances in the Relation between the Sexes', in *Sexuation*, ed. Renata Salecl (Durham, North Carolina: Duke University Press, 2000), cited from ms.

30. I am indebted for this material to the programme of the conference organised by the American Lacanian Link entitled 'The Other (That Does Not Exist)', taking place at the University of California at Irvine, Summer 2000.

31. Judith Butler, *Bodies that Matter: On the Discursive Limits of 'Sex'* (New York and London: Routledge, 1993), pp. 234–5.

32. Jacques Derrida, 'Signature Event Context', in *A Derrida Reader: Between the Blinds*, ed. Peggy Kamuf (New York and London: Harvester-Wheatsheaf, 1991), pp. 80–111.

33. Lacan, 1977b, p. 54.

34. Janet Bergstrom and Mary Ann Doane, *The Spectatrix*, special edition of *Camera Obscura*, 20–21 (1989).

35. Christian Metz, *Psychoanalysis and Cinema: The Imaginary Signifier* (London: Macmillan, 1982).

36. Lacan, 1977b, p. 195.

37. For further elaboration, see Dylan Evans, *An Introductory Dictionary of Lacanian Psychoanalysis* (London and New York: Routledge, 1996), pp. 72–3.

38. Laura Mulvey, 'Visual Pleasure and Narrative Cinema', in *Visual and Other Pleasures* (Basingstoke: Macmillan, 1989), pp. 14–26.

39. Ibid., pp. 18–19.

40. Vicki Lebeau, *Lost Angels: Psychoanalysis and Cinema* (London and New York: Routledge, 1995), p. 38.

41. In her article, 'The Orthopsychic Subject: Film Theory and the Reception of Lacan', in Joan Copjec, *Read my Desire: Lacan against the Historicists* (Cambridge, Massachusetts: MIT Press, 1994), pp. 15–38.

42. Copjec, p. 17.

43. Michel Foucault, *Power/Knowledge: Selected Interviews and Other Writings, 1972–1977* (Brighton: Harvester, 1980), pp. 146–56.

44. Lacan, 1977b, p. 102.

45. Copjec, p. 35.

46. Lebeau, p. 42.

47. For my brief account of *noir* criticism I draw on Elizabeth Cowie, '*Film noir* and women', in *Shades of*

Noir, ed. Joan Copjec (London and New York: Verso, 1993), pp. 121–65, and Mary Ann Doane, *Femmes Fatales: Feminism, Film Theory, Psychoanalysis* (New York and London: Routledge, 1991).

48. Doane, 1991, p. 2.

49. Toril Moi, *What is a Woman? and Other Essays* (Oxford: Oxford University Press, 1999).

50. Cited in Moi, p. 59.

Bibliography

Adams, Parveen. 'Waiving the Phallus'. *Differences*, 4:1 (1992), pp. 78–83.

Apter, Emily. 'Masquerade', in *Feminism and Psychoanalysis: A Critical Dictionary*. Elizabeth Wright, ed. Oxford: Blackwell, 1999. pp. 242–4.

Baruch, Elaine Hoffman and Serrano, Lucienne J. *Women Analyze Women: In France, England and the United States*. New York and London: Harvester-Wheatsheaf, 1988.

Bergstrom, Janet and Doane, Mary Ann. *The Spectatrix*, special edition of *Camera Obscura*, 20–21 (1989).

Brooks, Ann. *Postfeminisms: Feminism, Cultural Theory and Cultural Forms*. London and New York: Routledge, 1997.

Butler, Judith. *Bodies that Matter: On the Discursive Limits of 'Sex'*. New York and London: Routledge, 1993.

———. *The Psychic Life of Power: Theories in Subjection*. Stanford, California: Stanford University Press, 1997.

Cixous, Hélène and Clément, Catherine. *The Newly Born Woman*. Betsy Wing, trans. Manchester: Manchester University Press, 1986.

Copjec, Joan. 'The Orthopsychic Subject: Film Theory and the Reception of Lacan', in *Read my Desire: Lacan against the Historicists*. Cambridge, Massachusetts: MIT Press, 1994, pp. 15–38.

Cowie, Elizabeth. '*Film noir* and women', in *Shades of Noir*. Joan Copjec, ed. London and New York: Verso, 1993, pp. 121–65.

Denfeld, Rene. *The New Victorians: A Young Woman's Challenge to the Old Feminist Order*. London and New York: Simon and Schuster, 1995.

Derrida, Jacques. 'Signature Event Context', in *A Derrida Reader: Between the Blinds*. Peggy Kamuf, ed. New York and London: Harvester-Wheatsheaf, 1991.

Doane, Mary Ann. *Femmes Fatales: Feminism, Film Theory, Psychoanalysis*. New York and London: Routledge, 1991.

Evans, Dylan. *An Introductory Dictionary of Lacanian Psychoanalysis*. London and New York: Routledge, 1996.

Foucault, Michel. *Power/Knowledge: Selected Interviews and Other Writings, 1972–1977*. Brighton: Harvester, 1980.

Freud, Sigmund. *Totem and Taboo, Standard Edition of the Complete Psychological Works, Vol. XIII*. John Strachey, ed. and trans. London: Hogarth Press and the Institute of Psycho-Analysis (1940–68; *Totem and Taboo* originally published 1912), pp. 1–161.

Gamble, Sarah, ed. *The Icon Critical Dictionary of Feminism and Postfeminism*. Cambridge: Icon Books, 1999.

Gray, John. *Men are from Mars, Women are from Venus: A Practical Guide for Improving Communication and Getting What You Want in your Relationships*. New York: HarperCollins, 1992.

Kofman, Sarah. *The Enigma of Woman: Women in Freud's Writings*. Catherine Porter, trans. Ithaca and London: Cornell University Press, 1980.

Kristeva, Julia. *Black Sun: Depression and Melancholia*. New York: Columbia University Press, 1989.

Lacan, Jacques. *Écrits: A Selection*. Alan Sheridan, trans. London: Tavistock Publications, 1977a.

_____. *The Four Fundamental Concepts of Psycho-Analysis*. Alan Sheridan, trans., Jacques-Alain Miller, ed. London: Hogarth Press and the Institute of Psycho-Analysis, 1977b.

_____. *Television: A Challenge to the Psychoanalytic Establishment*. Jeffrey Mehlman, trans., Joan Copjec, ed. New York and London: W.W. Norton & Co., 1990.

_____. 'A Love Letter', in *The Seminar of Jacques Lacan: On Feminine Sexuality, the Limits of Love and Knowledge. Book XX. Encore: 1972–1973*. Bruce Fink, trans., Jacques-Alain Miller, ed. New York and London: W.W. Norton & Co., 1998, pp. 78–89.

Leader, Darian and Groves, Judy. *Introducing Lacan*. Cambridge: Icon Books, 2000.

Lebeau, Vicki. *Lost Angels: Psychoanalysis and Cinema*. London and New York: Routledge, 1995.

Metz, Christian. *Psychoanalysis and Cinema: The Imaginary Signifier.* London: Macmillan, 1982.

Miller, Jacques-Alain. 'On Semblances in the Relation between the Sexes', in *Sexuation.* Renata Salecl, ed. Durham, North Carolina: Duke University Press, 2000.

Mitchell, Juliet and Rose, Jacqueline. *Jacques Lacan and the* École Freudienne: *Feminine Sexuality.* Jacqueline Rose, trans. London and Basingstoke: Macmillan, 1982.

Moi, Toril. *What is a Woman? and Other Essays.* Oxford: Oxford University Press, 1999.

Mulvey, Laura. 'Visual Pleasure and Narrative Cinema', in *Visual and Other Pleasures.* Basingstoke: Macmillan, 1989, pp. 14–26.

Palomera, Vincente. 'Womanliness as a Masquerade'. *Lacanian Ink*, 5 (1992), pp. 43–51.

Raphael-Leff, Joan and Perelberg, Rosine Jozef, eds. *Female Experience: Three Generations of British Women Psychoanalysts on Work with Women.* London and New York: Routledge, 1997.

Riviere, Joan. 'Womanliness as a Masquerade'. *International Journal of Psycho-Analysis*, 8 (1929), pp. 303–13.

Russell, Bertrand. *The Principles of Mathematics.* London: Allen and Unwin, 1903.

Saussure, Ferdinand de. *Course in General Linguistics.* Wade Baskin, trans., Charles Bally and Albert Sechehaye, eds. London: Fontana/Collins, 1977.

Silverman, Kaja. 'The Lacanian Phallus'. *Differences*, 4:1 (1992), pp. 84–115.

Žižek, Slavoj. *The Indivisible Remainder: An Essay on Schelling and Related Matters*. London and New York: Verso, 1996.

Key terms

desire

Together with Freud, Lacan gives this term in psycho-analytic theory an entirely technical sense in which it departs from the common meaning, in that desire is understood as unconscious. A child may say it desires food, but this conscious use of the term expressing a need in the form of demand, is not desire in the psychoanalytic sense. Desire is rather primarily a desire for love, to be shown essentially in a *recognition of one's identity* by the Other. It is therefore designated as 'the desire of the Other'.

imaginary

This is one of Lacan's three 'orders' – imaginary, symbolic and real – which cannot be simply mapped onto Freud's tripartite structural model of ego, id and superego. They offer psychoanalytic theory a new classificatory system, in which all three are interdependent. The imaginary stems from the first identifications the child makes in the mirror-stage, in which it patterns its ego upon an imaginary counterpart that appears to offer the unity, cohesion and integrity that is never to be attained by the ego. The imaginary is therefore essentially narcissistic, and thus contains a recurrently aggressive element that shows itself each time the subject discovers itself to be fragmentary and not whole.

jouissance

The French word *jouissance* (roughly, 'enjoyment') is retained, not so much because it is hard to translate, but because Lacan has given it a special sense. In his early work, it meant 'enjoyment', specifically sexual enjoyment, but it came to be used for *drive satisfaction*, a satisfaction that is beyond Freud's pleasure principle. It appears in the suffering of a symptom, in psychic pain, as much as in pleasure, and thus partakes of an unconscious masochistic character. *Jouissance* is also opposed to lack. It initiates the fantasy that aims at recovering the primal loss, and therefore has a basis in the *real*, another of Lacan's three orders. In feminist discourses, the term has come to designate an additional, specifically feminine form of enjoyment (a non-phallic *jouissance*), which, in Lacan's sexuation graphs, is also open to men, if they 'choose' to insert themselves on the right-hand side.

lack

Lack is the effect of the primal separation from the mother's body, retrospectively experienced as the first castration consequent upon the subject's entry into language, which is already lying in wait for it. It produces desire for the unattainable lost object, which Lacan theorises as the 'object *a*'. It also represents the lack in the Other, the ultimate inadequacy of the symbolic order.

language

Language is central to Lacan's psychoanalysis. Freud had already placed language at the core of his practice, the 'talking cure'. For Lacan, language is the complex means of subject construction. For language in general he used the term *'langage'*; for the invasions of would-be articulate speech by poetic, emotive elements he coined the term *'lalangue'*, exemplified by his own provoking rhetoric in which thoughts never stop breaking through.

Name-of-the-Father

Lacan speaks of the symbolic order as upheld by a 'symbolic father' (the 'Name-of-the-Father') which is a metaphor for that which imposes the castration of language and stands for the ideal exigency of the law. Typically, he punned on this term, making it the *nom/non du père,* the 'name/no of the Father', in order to emphasise its symbolic barring function, $. Feminists who have championed Melanie Klein for her stress on the pre-Oedipal have refused Lacan's point that the Oedipus is always already there in the discourse of its parents even before the child is born.

object *a*

The entrance into language produces the separation from the primordial lost thing, the mother, an experience of loss driven by the fact that the attempts of the symbolic to bring the real within its boundaries always leave a hidden remainder which endlessly reinscribes the failure to achieve identity. To hide this failure, which the symbolic ignores, the subject pursues a fantasy of a lost object, the object *a*. A particular thing or happening in the subject's very early life starts the fantasy off, which offers the illusion of what will finally make up for the lack. Lacan noted from clinical practice that desire unconsciously swerves from the actual attainment of its end, preferring to repeat the approach to it continually.

other/Other

The first 'other' stands for the image that the child sees in the mirror, the flattering picture of wholeness that belies the actual fragmentary nature of the subject. This narcissistic completeness nevertheless is what enables the subject to found an ego, since it provides a fiction of control and mastery that works as its basis. The image becomes aggressive when other small others compete with it. The 'Other' stands for the symbolic itself, the presupposed locus of all desire, determining the speaking subject. It is not the person spoken to. Because for the subject the Other is taken to be the ultimate pole of the address, its lack is hidden, and Lacan writes it with the bar through it, 'Ⱥ'.

phallus

The phallus is paradoxically a signifier both of lack and of desire. The child first believes that the mother has the phallus, but in the course of the castration complex s/he escapes from absorption with the mother and comes to see the phallus as desired by the mother also. The phallus takes a fourth place in the Oedipal triangle, in this case an 'imaginary phallus' that the mother desires, for which the child endeavours to substitute itself. The symbolic father's intervention breaks up this collusion, substituting the 'symbolic phallus', as the acceptance of the father's prohibition. The penis retains a place in Lacanian theory as the 'real phallus', making its appearance as that which, in infantile masturbation, provokes the anxiety that heralds the assumption of castration. The loss of the maternal phallus continues to dominate fantasy, pursued as the lost object. For the man, the fantasy is wishing *to have* the phallus (powerful enough for the woman to comply with his fantasy); for the woman, *to be* the phallus (powerful enough to arouse the man's fantasy). Each can only take their place in the symbolic if they renounce these imaginary positions and instead adopt symbolic ones. For the man, the phallus is always beyond reach, locked up in his fantasy; for the woman, there is the option of experimentation with masquerade. The failure of this collusive manoeuvre leads Lacan to his dictum that 'there is no sexual relationship'.

72

real

The real is that which the symbolic is never able to capture by means of its binary differences. It is not the 'reality' of everyday objects and persons, but rather that which lies outside these familiar identifications. For the subject, it is that within and without which unconsciously resists the imposed definitions and leaves him/her with a troubling excess of *jouissance*.

signifier

In contrast to Saussure, Lacan maintains that the signifier is primary and produces the signified. He holds to Saussure's notion of the signifier as determined by its place in an order of differences, a closed and intrinsically meaningless set of material units in fixed logical relations. As regards speech itself, these units are made up of a limited group of phonemes, empty sound-images. The signifiers nevertheless lay down the boundaries that constitute the subject's unconscious. It must be stressed that the term 'signifier' is wider than that of 'word', because it includes all the symbolic elements that make up the communications of a society: gestures, facial expressions, signs, emblems, even objects themselves. What is important is what happens in the gaps between signifiers, that which cannot be said, because this testifies to the split between the one who speaks (the ego) and the one who is spoken about (the subject), and reminds us that as speaking beings we are alienated in language, although this is the only way in which we can create a social bond.

subject

The Lacanian subject is split, as distinct from the humanist ego, which is seen as single, sovereign and undivided. The entrance into language crucially produces the division between the subject of the unconscious which stumbles, and the conscious ego that considers itself as wholly invested in what it speaks. On the contrary, what the subject says and what is said, the 'statement' and the 'enunciation', never match. A real fragmentation confronts an illusory wholeness lingering in the imaginary. The subject is bound to the symbolic, while the ego cannot escape its imaginary origin. Lacan thus rejects those psychoanalytic theories that endeavour to restore a controlling ego, and instead sees the aim of analysis as the enhancement of the subject's awareness of its own divisions.

symbolic

The symbolic order for Lacan is that pre-existing order of language and law which forms the ground for the emergence of the subject. Its pre-established linguistic and cultural rules provide the distinctions that create the subject from the chaos of early experience, but also impose the castration that marks the subject as irremediably split, unable to link its imaginary identifications, the real that invades them, and the demands of the symbolic law.

unconscious

The unconscious for Freud was initially the repository of what is repressed out of the conscious mind, and so accessible only through its indirect effects such as dreams, symptoms and slips. Later, in his tripartite scheme of superego, ego and id, he preferred to place unconscious elements in all three. Lacan maintains that these indirect effects are the marks of the signifiers of language. They are not only what brings the unconscious into being, but they are responsible for structuring it in ways similar to that of language itself. Lacan asserts this with his dictum that 'the unconscious is structured like a language'. He calls it the effects of the signifier on the subject, in that the repressed signifiers return in the formations of the unconscious. Because of this effect of the signifier impinging on the subject, as if from outside, 'the unconscious is the discourse of the Other'.

Other titles available in the Postmodern Encounters series from Icon/Totem

Derrida and the End of History
Stuart Sim

ISBN 1 84046 094 6
UK £2.99   USA $7.95

What does it mean to proclaim 'the end of history', as several thinkers have done in recent years? Francis Fukuyama, the American political theorist, created a considerable stir in *The End of History and the Last Man* (1992) by claiming that the fall of communism and the triumph of free market liberalism brought an 'end of history' as we know it. Prominent among his critics has been the French philosopher Jacques Derrida, whose *Specters of Marx* (1993) deconstructed the concept of 'the end of history' as an ideological confidence trick, in an effort to salvage the unfinished and ongoing project of democracy.

Derrida and the End of History places Derrida's claim within the context of a wider tradition of 'endist' thought. Derrida's critique of endism is highlighted as one of his most valuable contributions to the postmodern cultural debate – as well as being the most accessible entry to *deconstruction*, the controversial philosophical movement founded by him.

Stuart Sim is Professor of English Studies at the University of Sunderland. The author of several works on critical and cultural theory, he edited *The Icon Critical Dictionary of Postmodern Thought* (1998).

Foucault and Queer Theory
Tamsin Spargo
ISBN 1 84046 092 X
UK £2.99   USA $7.95

Michel Foucault is the most gossiped-about celebrity of
French poststructuralist theory. The homophobic insult
'queer' is now proudly reclaimed by some who once
called themselves lesbian or gay. What is the connection
between the two?

This is a postmodern encounter between Foucault's
theories of sexuality, power and discourse and the
current key exponents of queer thinking who have
adopted, revised and criticised Foucault. Our
understanding of gender, identity, sexuality and cultural
politics will be radically altered in this meeting of
transgressive figures.

Foucault and Queer Theory excels as a brief introduction
to Foucault's compelling ideas and the development of
queer culture with its own outspoken views on
heteronormativity, sado-masochism, performativity,
transgender, the end of gender, liberation-versus-
difference, late capitalism and the impact of AIDS on
theories and practices.

Tamsin Spargo worked as an actor before taking up her
current position as Senior Lecturer in Literary and
Historical Studies at Liverpool John Moores University.
She writes on religious writing, critical and cultural
theory and desire.

Nietzsche and Postmodernism
Dave Robinson
ISBN 1 84046 093 8
UK £2.99   USA $7.95

Friedrich Nietzsche (1844–1900) has exerted a huge
influence on 20th century philosophy and literature – an
influence that looks set to continue into the 21st century.
Nietzsche questioned what it means for us to live in our
modern world. He was an 'anti-philosopher' who
expressed grave reservations about the reliability and
extent of human knowledge. His radical scepticism
disturbs our deepest-held beliefs and values. For these
reasons, Nietzsche casts a 'long shadow' on the complex
cultural and philosophical phenomenon we now call
'postmodernism'.

Nietzsche and Postmodernism explains the key ideas of
this 'Anti-Christ' philosopher. It then provides a clear
account of the central themes of postmodernist thought
exemplified by such thinkers as Derrida, Foucault,
Lyotard and Rorty, and concludes by asking if Nietzsche
can justifiably be called the first great postmodernist.

Dave Robinson has taught philosophy for many years. He
is the author of Icon/Totem's introductory guides to
Philosophy, Ethics and Descartes. He thinks that
Nietzsche is a postmodernist, but he's not sure.

Baudrillard and the Millennium
Christopher Horrocks

ISBN 1 84046 091 1
UK £2.99   USA $7.95

'In a sense, we do not believe in the Year 2000', says French thinker Jean Baudrillard. Still more disturbing is his claim that the millennium might not take place. Baudrillard's analysis of 'Y2K' reveals a repentant culture intent on storing, mourning and laundering its past, and a world from which even the possibility of the 'end of history' has vanished. Yet behind this bleak vision of integrated reality, Baudrillard identifies enigmatic possibilities and perhaps a final ironic twist.

Baudrillard and the Millennium confronts the strategies of this major cultural analyst's encounter with the greatest non-event of the postmodern age, and accounts for the critical censure of Baudrillard's enterprise. Key topics, such as natural catastrophes, the body, 'victim culture', identity and Internet viruses, are discussed in reference to the development of Jean Baudrillard's millenarian thought from the 1980s to the threshold of the Year 2000 – from simulation to disappearance.

Christopher Horrocks is Senior Lecturer in Art History at Kingston University in Surrey. His publications include *Introducing Baudrillard* and *Introducing Foucault*, both published by Icon/Totem. He lives in Tulse Hill, in the south of London.